Motherhood 101

Inspiration and Wisdom to Help You Become A Great Mom

by

Cheri Fuller

Tulsa, Oklahoma

3rd Printing

Motherhood 101
Inspiration and Wisdom to Help You Become a Great Mom
ISBN 1-56292-269-6
Copyright © 1997 by Cheri Fuller
P.O. Box 770493
Oklahoma City, OK 73177
"Published in association with the literary agency of Alive Communications, Inc.,
1465 Kelly Johnson Blvd., Suite 320, Colorado Springs, CO 80920."
Published by Honor Books, Inc.
P.O. Box 55388
Tulsa, Oklahoma 74155

Introduction

Most of us mothers are extremely busy making a home for our families, cooking, carpooling, and some are juggling an in-home business or an out-of-the-home job. Many are homeschooling their children, and lots of others volunteer at their kids' schools. Perhaps, like me, on many days you find yourself short of time, but you still want to be the best mother you can be. That's where this book will come in handy, giving gems of wisdom, wit, and encouragement on the subject that is close to our hearts — being a mom!

In the pages ahead you will find inspiring quotes and Scripture on all the issues which affect motherhood. Then, following the quote is a practical application on the subject. There is humor to lighten your load, and pithy sayings by some very wise women and gentlemen. (We wouldn't want to leave the men out!)

Many of these insightful statements have been on my bulletin board or refrigerator, and have proven to be particularly helpful in parenting my own three children through their growing-up years. Other quotes are from my speaking and writing. They will give you a bigger picture of a mother's journey. If you have younger children, and you find a quote more suited to an older child, enjoy it, and tuck it away for another day *that will be here before you know it*! Keep your own journal of "nuggets" on reflective questions, or just list things as you think of them: gifts and talents of each child, or blessings you have received.

Motherhood is a learning process, and as our children grow, we grow — day by day. When holding our "little ones" for the first time, we cannot fathom the wisdom, know-how, and patience that will be required. Through the years, our hearts are enlarged, and we grow in our relationships with others and God, Who gives us the strength, love, and perseverance we need for each day.

I hope this book will give you many practical and creative ideas, that it will encourage you in your quest to raise children with strong values and purpose — and that you will have *fun* along the way!

When you are feeding, teaching, nurturing, soothing hurts, cleaning up messes, and loving your children, remember that you are doing the most important job on earth — rearing the next generation! A hundred years from now, it won't matter how much money was in your checking account, what kind of house you lived in, or what car you drove, but the world will be different because you influenced the life of a child.

CHERI FULLER

*A*s we encourage our children, they will grow in confidence and become encouragers themselves. Someday, when you need it the most and least expect it, your son or daughter will come alongside and say just the right building-up words you need to keep going or to face a trial.

CHERI FULLER

"A word of encouragement does wonders!"
Proverbs 12:25

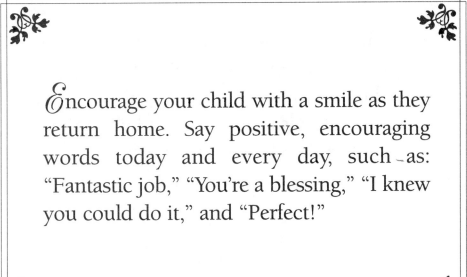

*E*ncourage your child with a smile as they return home. Say positive, encouraging words today and every day, such as: "Fantastic job," "You're a blessing," "I knew you could do it," and "Perfect!"

A hug can soothe a small child's pain
and bring a rainbow after rain.
The hug! There's just no doubt about it....
A hug delights and warms and charms,
it must be why God gave us arms.

ANONYMOUS

*"He took them [the children] in His arms
and began blessing them."*
Mark 10:16 NASB

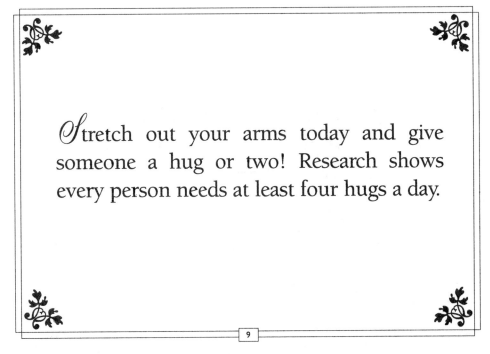

*S*tretch out your arms today and give someone a hug or two! Research shows every person needs at least four hugs a day.

*W*e do not fully appreciate
the love of our mothers for us
until we become mothers.

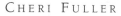

CHERI FULLER

"As a mother comforts her child, so will I comfort you."
Isaiah 66:13 NIV

*E*ven if it seems that no one notices your "labors of love," be assured that all the serving, loving, cooking, carpooling, and caring for your children is seen and appreciated by your heavenly Father. Wouldn't it be nice to write *your* mother a letter today thanking her for her character qualities, for all the cookies she baked, PTA meetings she attended, birthday parties she threw, and zany memories from your growing-up years.

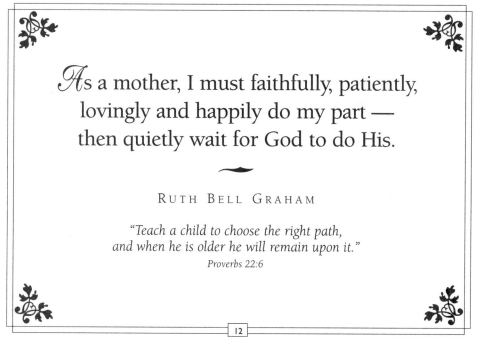

*A*s a mother, I must faithfully, patiently, lovingly and happily do my part — then quietly wait for God to do His.

RUTH BELL GRAHAM

*"Teach a child to choose the right path,
and when he is older he will remain upon it."*
Proverbs 22:6

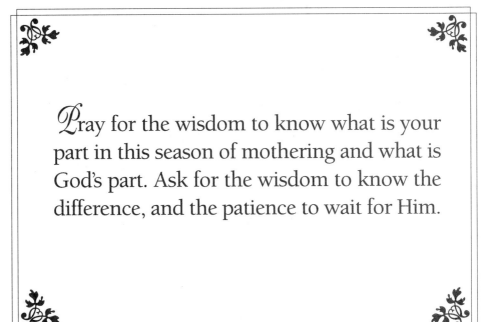

$\mathcal{P}$ray for the wisdom to know what is your part in this season of mothering and what is God's part. Ask for the wisdom to know the difference, and the patience to wait for Him.

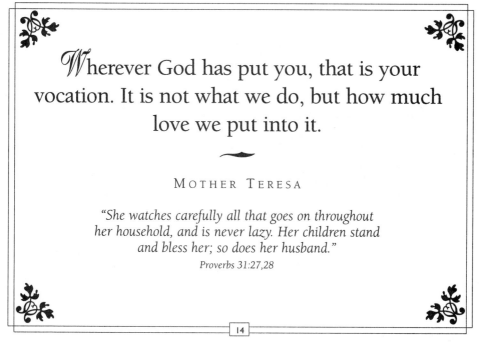

Wherever God has put you, that is your vocation. It is not what we do, but how much love we put into it.

MOTHER TERESA

"She watches carefully all that goes on throughout her household, and is never lazy. Her children stand and bless her; so does her husband."
Proverbs 31:27,28

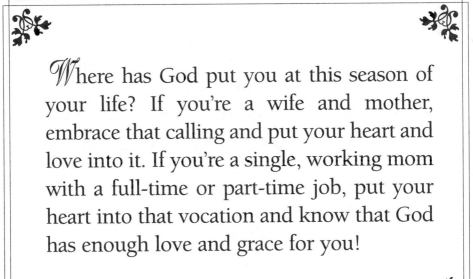

*W*here has God put you at this season of your life? If you're a wife and mother, embrace that calling and put your heart and love into it. If you're a single, working mom with a full-time or part-time job, put your heart into that vocation and know that God has enough love and grace for you!

Only the open gate can receive visitors.
Only the open hand can receive gifts.
Only the open mind can receive wisdom.
Only the open heart can receive love.

JOAN WALSH ANGLUND

*"Cheerfully share your home with those who need
a meal or a place to stay for the night."*
1 Peter 4:9

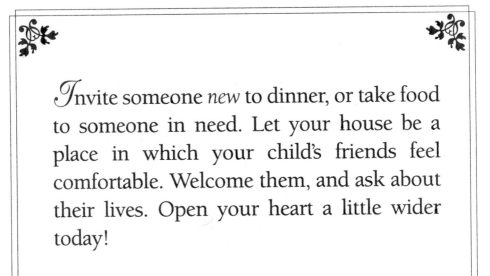

Invite someone *new* to dinner, or take food to someone in need. Let your house be a place in which your child's friends feel comfortable. Welcome them, and ask about their lives. Open your heart a little wider today!

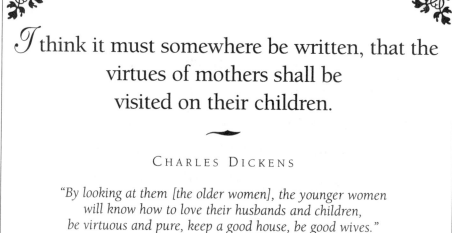

𝒥 think it must somewhere be written, that the virtues of mothers shall be visited on their children.

CHARLES DICKENS

*"By looking at them [the older women], the younger women
will know how to love their husbands and children,
be virtuous and pure, keep a good house, be good wives."*
Titus 2:3 MESSAGE

$\mathscr{F}$ind an "older woman," a woman farther along in the mothering journey than you are. Ask her to spend time with you as a mentor, encouraging you on how to be a godly wife and mother by sharing her wisdom and experience with you. If you know of a younger mother who needs such mentoring, take the initiative to reach out to her.

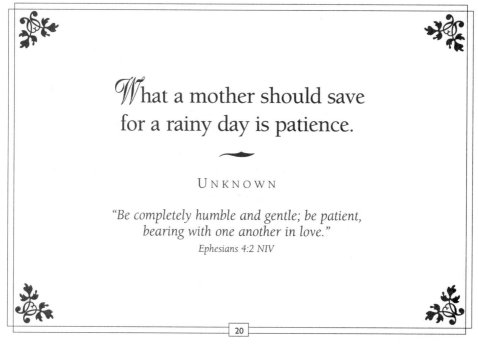

*W*hat a mother should save
for a rainy day is patience.

UNKNOWN

*"Be completely humble and gentle; be patient,
bearing with one another in love."*
Ephesians 4:2 NIV

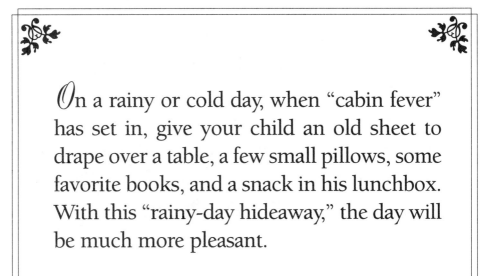

*O*n a rainy or cold day, when "cabin fever" has set in, give your child an old sheet to drape over a table, a few small pillows, some favorite books, and a snack in his lunchbox. With this "rainy-day hideaway," the day will be much more pleasant.

*M*y little Donny, while riding on my lap
in the front seat of the car said to me,
"Mommy, when I grow up, I'm going to
marry you." "Oh, honey, you can't do that.
I'm already married." "You are?" he asked. Twenty years
flew by. He married someone else. We have those
moments for such a short time.

THELMA AVORE

"Children are a gift from God; they are his reward."
Psalm 127:3

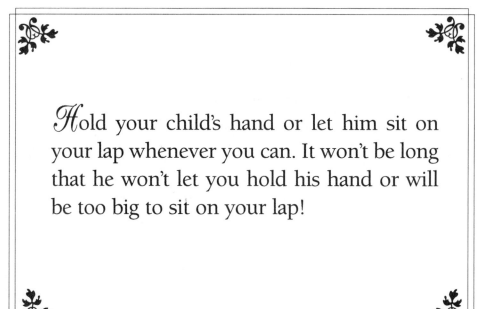

Hold your child's hand or let him sit on your lap whenever you can. It won't be long that he won't let you hold his hand or will be too big to sit on your lap!

*W*hy pray for their future husbands even while our daughters are little girls? Because somewhere in the world those future husbands...are little boys. With the pressures to conform to this world, those little boys need a lot of prayer.... Even though I don't even know who I'm praying for, God does.

AL MENCONI

"I prayed for this child, and the Lord has granted me what I asked of him."
1 Samuel 1:27 NIV

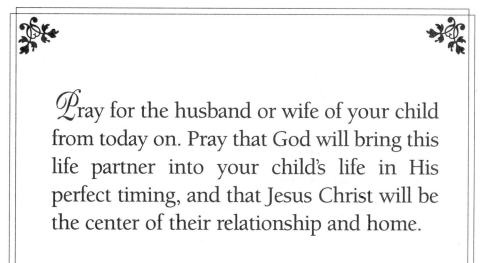

$\mathscr{P}$ray for the husband or wife of your child from today on. Pray that God will bring this life partner into your child's life in His perfect timing, and that Jesus Christ will be the center of their relationship and home.

Before a child can *say* kindness, he can understand the forgiving smile on his mother's face; before he can *spell* God, he can sense his mother's anxiety dissipate as she talks to Someone he cannot even see. Before he can *understand* the concept of love, he can snuggle near his mother's heart, closed in tight to the solid security of belonging.

JILL BRISCOE

"As water reflects a face, so a man's heart reflects the man."
Proverbs 27:19 NIV

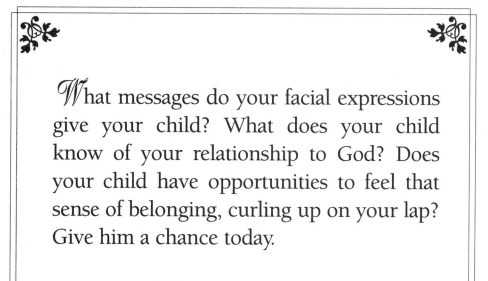

*W*hat messages do your facial expressions give your child? What does your child know of your relationship to God? Does your child have opportunities to feel that sense of belonging, curling up on your lap? Give him a chance today.

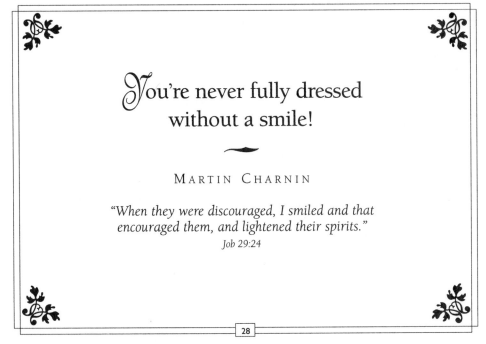

You're never fully dressed
without a smile!

MARTIN CHARNIN

*"When they were discouraged, I smiled and that
encouraged them, and lightened their spirits."*
Job 29:24

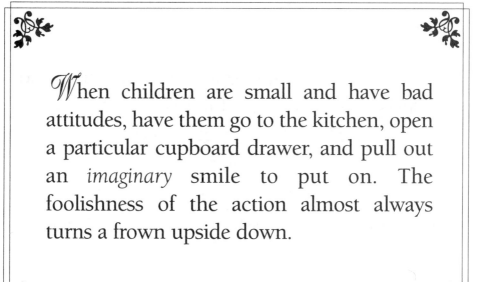

*W*hen children are small and have bad attitudes, have them go to the kitchen, open a particular cupboard drawer, and pull out an *imaginary* smile to put on. The foolishness of the action almost always turns a frown upside down.

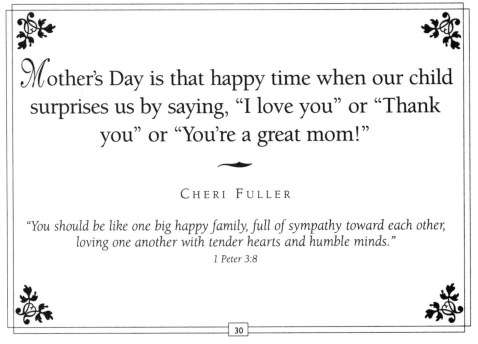

$\mathscr{M}$other's Day is that happy time when our child surprises us by saying, "I love you" or "Thank you" or "You're a great mom!"

CHERI FULLER

"You should be like one big happy family, full of sympathy toward each other, loving one another with tender hearts and humble minds."
1 Peter 3:8

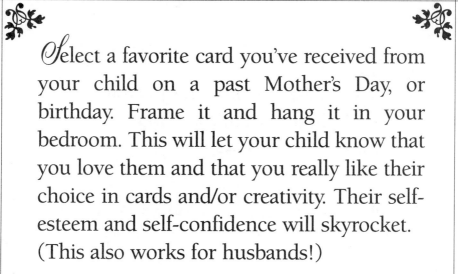

*S*elect a favorite card you've received from your child on a past Mother's Day, or birthday. Frame it and hang it in your bedroom. This will let your child know that you love them and that you really like their choice in cards and/or creativity. Their self-esteem and self-confidence will skyrocket. (This also works for husbands!)

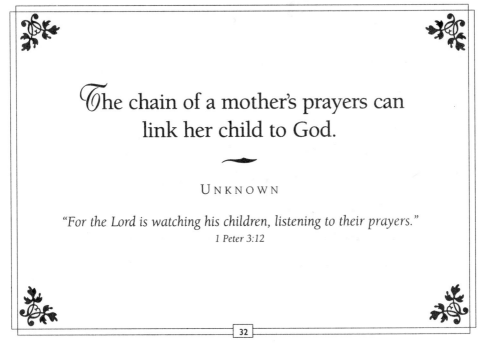

The chain of a mother's prayers can
link her child to God.

UNKNOWN

"For the Lord is watching his children, listening to their prayers."
1 Peter 3:12

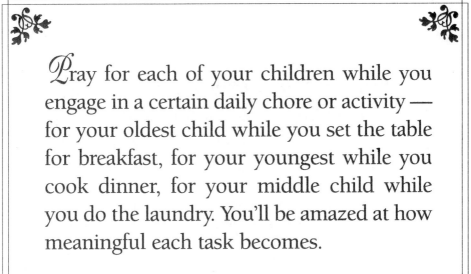

$\mathscr{P}$ray for each of your children while you engage in a certain daily chore or activity — for your oldest child while you set the table for breakfast, for your youngest while you cook dinner, for your middle child while you do the laundry. You'll be amazed at how meaningful each task becomes.

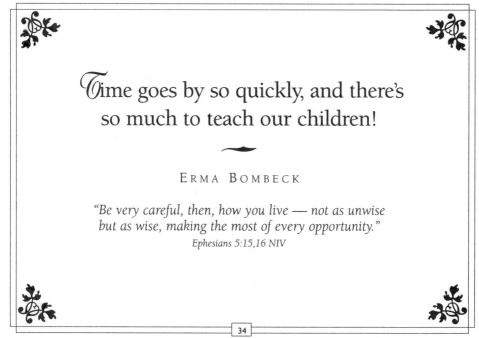

Time goes by so quickly, and there's so much to teach our children!

ERMA BOMBECK

*"Be very careful, then, how you live — not as unwise
but as wise, making the most of every opportunity."*
Ephesians 5:15,16 NIV

*W*atch for "teachable moments," those natural opportunities for talking with your child about your values, knowledge, and ideas; moments for encouraging their natural curiosity by answering their questions about why the clouds form and the lightning strikes.

You may have tangible wealth untold
caskets of jewels and coffers of gold.
Richer than I you can never be —
I had a mother who *read* to me.

STRICKLAND GILLILAN

"Teach believers with your life: by word, by demeanor,
by love, by faith, by integrity. Stay at your post reading
Scripture, giving counsel, teaching."
1 Timothy 4:12,13 MESSAGE

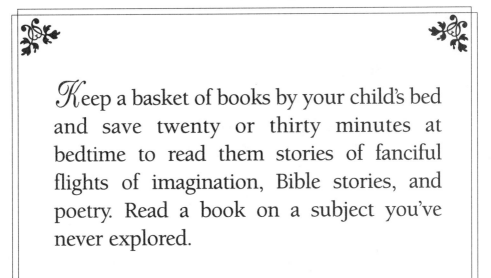

$\mathscr{K}$eep a basket of books by your child's bed and save twenty or thirty minutes at bedtime to read them stories of fanciful flights of imagination, Bible stories, and poetry. Read a book on a subject you've never explored.

The walks and talks we have with our two-year-olds in red boots have a great deal to do with the values they will cherish as adults.

Edith F. Hunter

"My steps have held closely to Your paths — to the tracks of the One Who has gone on before; my feet have not slipped."
Psalm 17:5 AMP

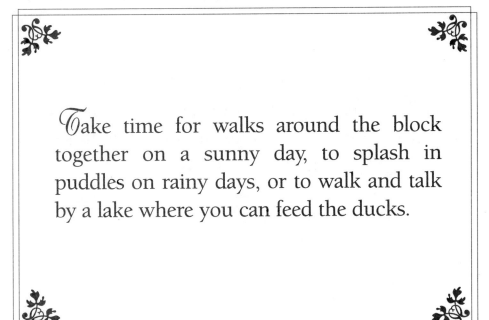

Take time for walks around the block together on a sunny day, to splash in puddles on rainy days, or to walk and talk by a lake where you can feed the ducks.

*L*ullaby CD's and other recorded music collections are great, but they can't replace a mother's voice as she sings her little one to sleep or soothes a fever.

CHERI FULLER

"Let them sing for joy as they lie upon their beds."
Psalm 149:5

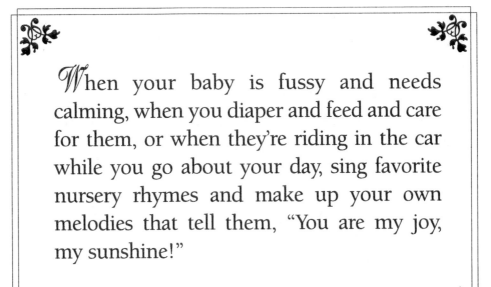

When your baby is fussy and needs calming, when you diaper and feed and care for them, or when they're riding in the car while you go about your day, sing favorite nursery rhymes and make up your own melodies that tell them, "You are my joy, my sunshine!"

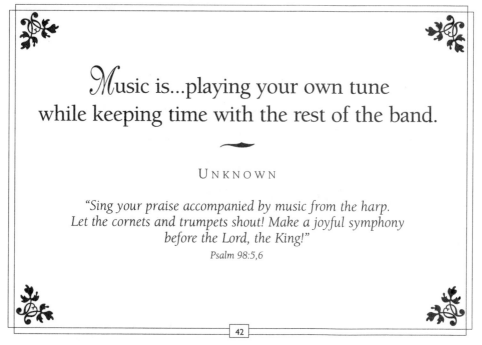

$\mathcal{M}$usic is...playing your own tune
while keeping time with the rest of the band.

UNKNOWN

"Sing your praise accompanied by music from the harp.
Let the cornets and trumpets shout! Make a joyful symphony
before the Lord, the King!"

Psalm 98:5,6

*M*ake music together by making rhythm instruments out of materials around the house: shakers, from rice in a plastic container with tight lid; clackers, from two wooden spoons; and drums, from a round oatmeal container. Play music and have your child beat time to the music. March to the music and have a ball together!

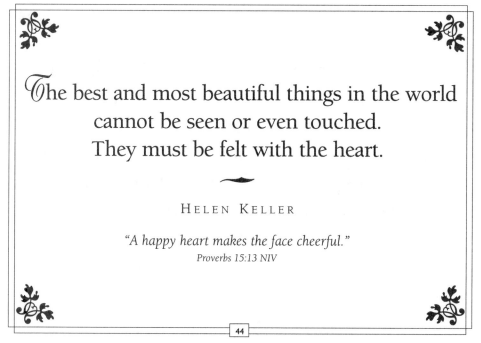

The best and most beautiful things in the world
cannot be seen or even touched.
They must be felt with the heart.

HELEN KELLER

"A happy heart makes the face cheerful."
Proverbs 15:13 NIV

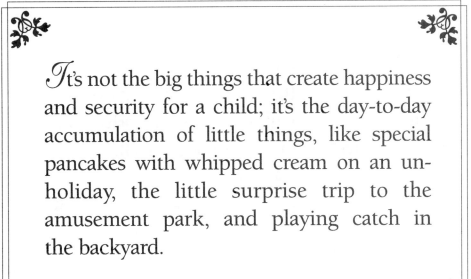

It's not the big things that create happiness and security for a child; it's the day-to-day accumulation of little things, like special pancakes with whipped cream on an un-holiday, the little surprise trip to the amusement park, and playing catch in the backyard.

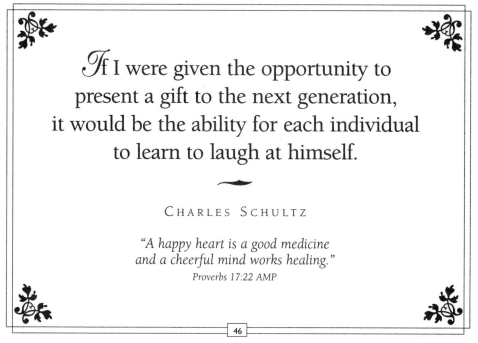

If I were given the opportunity to present a gift to the next generation, it would be the ability for each individual to learn to laugh at himself.

CHARLES SCHULTZ

"A happy heart is a good medicine and a cheerful mind works healing."
Proverbs 17:22 AMP

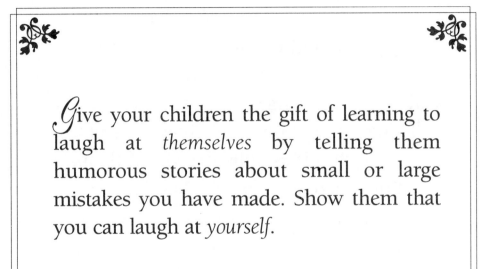

*G*ive your children the gift of learning to laugh at *themselves* by telling them humorous stories about small or large mistakes you have made. Show them that you can laugh at *yourself*.

*L*et the children laugh and be glad....
Allow them a genuine laughter now. Laugh
with them, till tears run down your faces —
till a memory of pure delight and precious
relationship is established within them,
indestructible, personal, and forever.

WALTER WANGERIN

"The LORD has done great things for us, and we are filled with joy."
Psalm 126:3 NIV

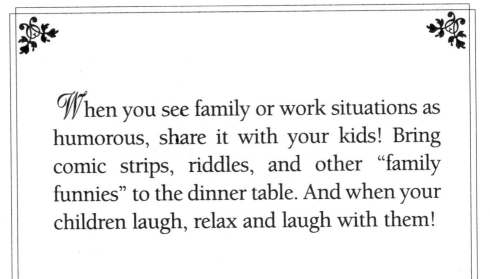

*W*hen you see family or work situations as humorous, share it with your kids! Bring comic strips, riddles, and other "family funnies" to the dinner table. And when your children laugh, relax and laugh with them!

Storytelling has great value for its own sake — the entertainment and sheer delight a well-told story can bring to a child. A story is a love-gift from parent to child, from grandparent to grandchild.

CHERI FULLER

"I will show you lessons from our history, stories handed down to us from former generations. I will reveal these truths to you so that you can describe these glorious deeds of Jehovah to your children."

Psalm 78:2-4

*W*hether serious (with a message or moral) or frivolous (totally silly), the most intriguing story to a small child is an imaginary one. Perhaps it could be made up of present experiences or the familiarity of the past. Of course, the most important feature of the tale is that it seems to be centered around a child who "miraculously" resembles the listener!

A baby is...

a kiss from heaven blown
from the hand of God.

an angel whose wings grow shorter
as their legs grow longer.

UNKNOWN (BOTH QUOTES)

*E*njoy your child's growing-up years.

- Take many photographs of your children — even of them sleeping (to remind you of those peaceful moments).

- Have a surprise teddy bear tea party, a picnic at a nearby lake or pond, or just serve a silly meal.

- Play one of their games with them or color a page in their coloring book.

The years speed by so quickly!

*C*hildren are like flowers — they need to be watered (praised), showered with sunshine (encouraged), and rooted in love (taught God's unconditional love through the love of their parents) in order to bloom.

TAMMY LOVELL

"If God gives such attention to the wildflowers, most of them never even seen, don't you think he'll attend to you, take pride in you, do his best for you?"
Luke 12:28 MESSAGE

$\mathcal{P}$raise your children for the inward qualities you want them to develop (joy, perseverance, kindness, etc.) not just for their outward successes. Let your encouragement be steady and warm them like a summer day. Root them in God's love, and trust Him to bring a bountiful harvest in their lives!

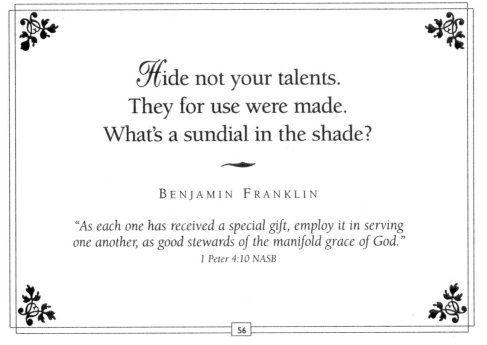

*H*ide not your talents.
They for use were made.
What's a sundial in the shade?

BENJAMIN FRANKLIN

*"As each one has received a special gift, employ it in serving
one another, as good stewards of the manifold grace of God."*
1 Peter 4:10 NASB

Look for your children's talents and let them know that what they do is important to you. Does he write poetry? You can say, "Let me read your newest poems." Does she paint, play tennis, or like to invent new gadgets? Encourage their developing skills and gifts, and give them opportunities to use them at home, church, and school.

*O*nly if a child's emotional tank is full
can he be expected to be his best
and do his best.

Dr. Ross Campbell

*"If you love someone you will be loyal to him no matter what the cost.
You will always believe in him, always expect the best of him,
and always stand your ground in defending him."*
1 Corinthians 13:7

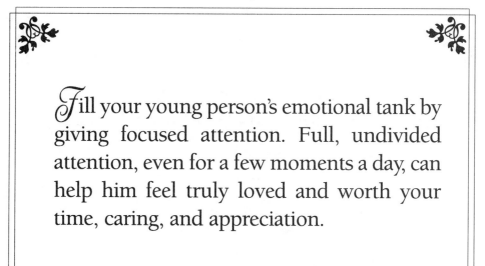

*F*ill your young person's emotional tank by giving focused attention. Full, undivided attention, even for a few moments a day, can help him feel truly loved and worth your time, caring, and appreciation.

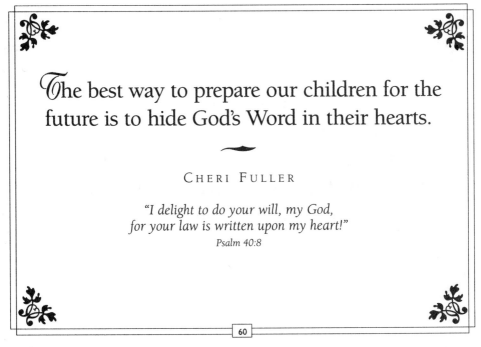

The best way to prepare our children for the future is to hide God's Word in their hearts.

CHERI FULLER

*"I delight to do your will, my God,
for your law is written upon my heart!"*
Psalm 40:8

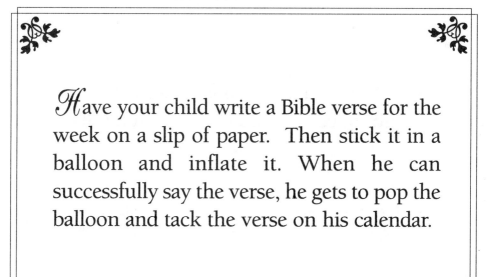

*H*ave your child write a Bible verse for the week on a slip of paper. Then stick it in a balloon and inflate it. When he can successfully say the verse, he gets to pop the balloon and tack the verse on his calendar.

*C*hildren are islands of curiosity
surrounded by a sea of question marks.

UNKNOWN

*"But if any of you lacks wisdom, let him ask of God, who gives to all
men generously and without reproach, and it will be given to him."*
James 1:5 NASB

When your child asks a question, show enthusiasm! If you don't know the answer or don't have a book to look it up, write it on an index card (keep a stack on the kitchen counter). Next time you and your child are close to the library, take the question card and discover the answer together!

Never wait for a fitter time or place
to talk to God. To wait till you go to church
or to your closet is to make Him wait.
He will listen as you walk.

GEORGE MACDONALD

*"Blessed are those who have learned to acclaim you, who walk in the light
of your presence, O LORD. They rejoice in your name all day long."*
Psalm 89:15,16 NIV

Take a prayer walk around the block. Talk to God about each of your children, your husband, and your own concerns. Continue your dialogue with Him as you walk through the rest of your day, as you work and care for your family. Know that He can be worshipped through any of the tasks you commit to Him.

The kind word spoken today will likely bear its fruit tomorrow.

CHERI FULLER

"Never forget to be truthful and kind. Hold these virtues tightly.
Write them deep within your heart."
Proverbs 3:3

*R*emember and notice the good things your child does. In place of critical words, try substituting phrases (on a regular basis), such as, "You really are growing up" or "You're doing a great job on your homework," or "I really appreciate your (humor, perseverance, kindness)." Then watch your children's motivation and confidence rise!

*M*y mother came to all my performances. She'd lead the laughter and applause. If anybody spoke too loudly or coughed, my mother shushed them with an iron stare.

MILTON BERLE

"Don't just think about your own affairs, but be interested in others, too, and in what they are doing."
Philippians 2:4

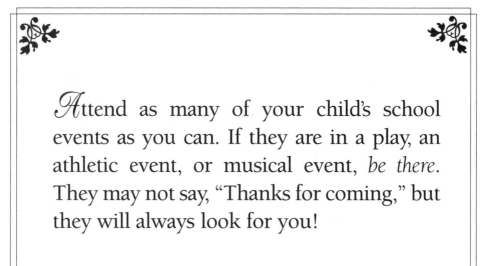

*A*ttend as many of your child's school events as you can. If they are in a play, an athletic event, or musical event, *be there*. They may not say, "Thanks for coming," but they will always look for you!

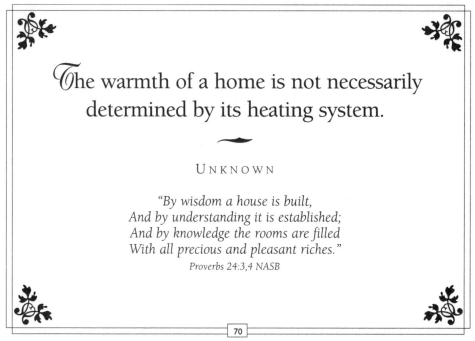

*T*he warmth of a home is not necessarily determined by its heating system.

UNKNOWN

"By wisdom a house is built,
And by understanding it is established;
And by knowledge the rooms are filled
With all precious and pleasant riches."
Proverbs 24:3,4 NASB

*I*ncrease the warmth in your home by more hugs and physical affection, more praise and positive comments, and more prayer and laughter.

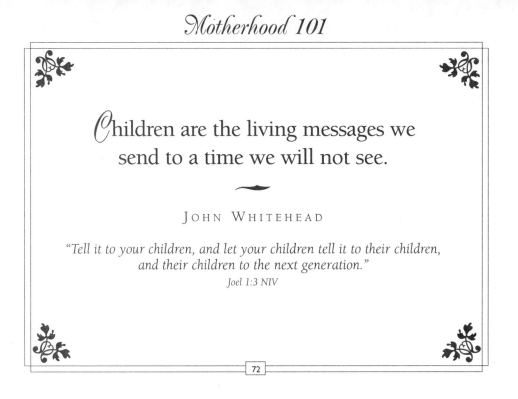

Children are the living messages we
send to a time we will not see.

JOHN WHITEHEAD

*"Tell it to your children, and let your children tell it to their children,
and their children to the next generation."*
Joel 1:3 NIV

$\mathcal{K}$eep family traditions throughout the year, such as, reading the Christmas story from the Bible, making a special cake for birthdays with a note signed by each family member expressing appreciation for the birthday person, or decorating the Christmas tree the day after Thanksgiving. Traditions not only pass on important values and beliefs to your child, they also tie your family together from generation to generation.

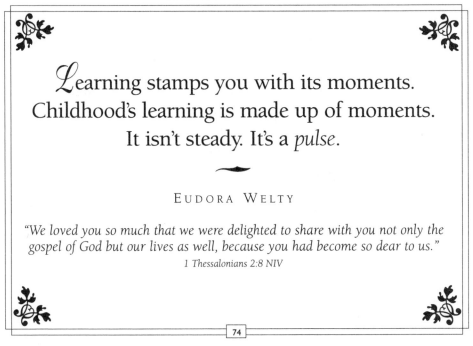

*L*earning stamps you with its moments.
Childhood's learning is made up of moments.
It isn't steady. It's a *pulse*.

EUDORA WELTY

"We loved you so much that we were delighted to share with you not only the gospel of God but our lives as well, because you had become so dear to us."
1 Thessalonians 2:8 NIV

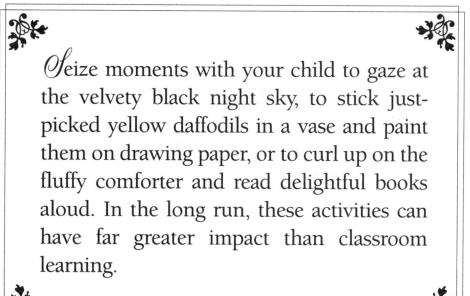

Seize moments with your child to gaze at the velvety black night sky, to stick just-picked yellow daffodils in a vase and paint them on drawing paper, or to curl up on the fluffy comforter and read delightful books aloud. In the long run, these activities can have far greater impact than classroom learning.

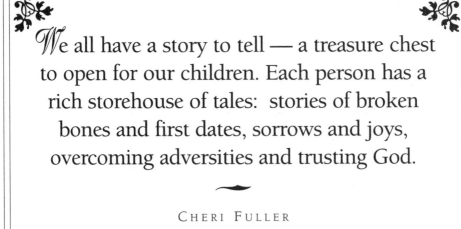

We all have a story to tell — a treasure chest to open for our children. Each person has a rich storehouse of tales: stories of broken bones and first dates, sorrows and joys, overcoming adversities and trusting God.

CHERI FULLER

"It is a wonderful heritage to have an honest father [and mother]."
Proverbs 20:7

*U*se trips and errand time in the car to tell your child stories of your own childhood:

- mischief and misadventures you got into
- your first stitches or black eye
- when you first accepted Jesus into your life
- your first camp experience
- the first Christmas you remember

A promise should be given with
caution and kept with care.

UNKNOWN

*"One who doesn't give the gift he promised is like a cloud blowing
over a desert without dropping any rain."*
Proverbs 25:14

Think it over before you promise your child an activity or reward. Can you deliver? Then keep your promise — even if it's inconvenient — and you will build in him a strong sense of trust.

"What's it like to raise a teenager?" a parent once asked me. "Well," I replied, "do you remember what your toddler was like when he went through the terrible-twos stage? Just multiply that by eight and add a driver's license!"

LIZ TARPY

*"For You are my hope; O Lord God, You are my trust
from my youth and the source of my confidence."*
Psalm 71:5 AMP

Although parenting teenagers is a challenge, it can also be great fun if we occasionally take time to meet them on their turf. Take your teen out (or better yet, let them drive you!) for a hamburger, to shoot a few hoops, or go to an art museum. The main thing is to enjoy time together and talk about whatever is on their mind.

A little bit of boredom in your child's life
is not the end of the world. It might lead
to their thinking creatively or discovering
a wonderful idea in a new book.

CHERI FULLER

*"No eye has seen, no ear has heard, no mind has conceived what God has
prepared for those who love him — but God has revealed it to us by his Spirit."*
1 Corinthians 2:9,10 NIV

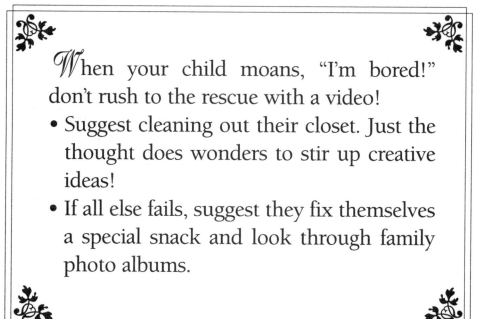

When your child moans, "I'm bored!" don't rush to the rescue with a video!

- Suggest cleaning out their closet. Just the thought does wonders to stir up creative ideas!
- If all else fails, suggest they fix themselves a special snack and look through family photo albums.

I'm so glad Corrie ten Boom passed on to us moms and grandmothers God's private telephone number — JE 333, for Jeremiah 33:3 — and it's available to His children 24 hours of every day. You just have to "call to Him, and He will answer you and He will tell you great and mighty things which you do not know."

CHERI FULLER

$\mathcal{D}$ial the Lord's private telephone number today and every day when you have concerns about your child or when you need wisdom for the decisions and challenges you face. He loves to hear from you when you pray!

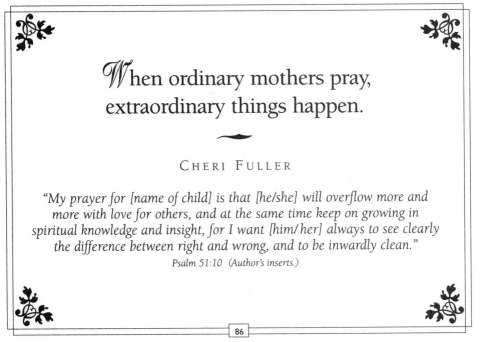

When ordinary mothers pray,
extraordinary things happen.

CHERI FULLER

*"My prayer for [name of child] is that [he/she] will overflow more and
more with love for others, and at the same time keep on growing in
spiritual knowledge and insight, for I want [him/her] always to see clearly
the difference between right and wrong, and to be inwardly clean."*
Psalm 51:10 (Author's inserts.)

*N*ever give up hope and never stop praying for your children. Pray specifically that God will:

- give them a hunger for righteousness,
- allow them to see the deceptions of Satan,
- flood them with friends who will influence them positively for God, and
- empower you with His unconditional love, trust, and understanding.

Personalize your prayers by putting your child's name in a Scripture passage that communicates your hopes and desires for them.

$\mathcal{S}$elf-confidence is a person's trust in his or her own abilities to handle situations, solve problems, deal with others effectively, and complete tasks.

RICHARD BAUMAN

"A righteous man may have many troubles, but the LORD delivers him from them all."
Psalm 34:19 NIV

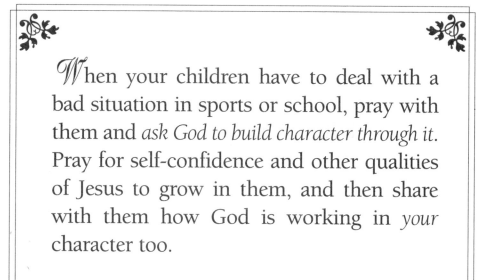

*W*hen your children have to deal with a bad situation in sports or school, pray with them and *ask God to build character through it.* Pray for self-confidence and other qualities of Jesus to grow in them, and then share with them how God is working in *your* character too.

$\mathcal{C}$hildren need friends who will affirm and support them. They also need to see that friendship is like a checking account, and only works if they continue to make deposits.

CHERI FULLER

"A true friend is always loyal."
Proverbs 17:17

The art of making and keeping friends is demonstrated to your child as they see your friendships grow through the years. In order to increase their awareness of friendly deposits into another human being, encourage them to:

- Invite a classmate over for a planned activity.
- Attend church classes and activities with their peers.
- Listen to their friend to find out what they like.
- Make haste in apologizing, and forgive quickly.
- Be loyal and don't tell the secrets shared.

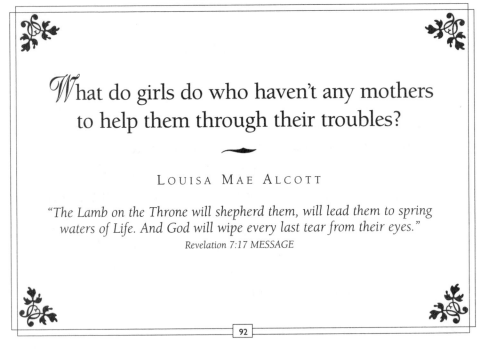

What do girls do who haven't any mothers
to help them through their troubles?

LOUISA MAE ALCOTT

*"The Lamb on the Throne will shepherd them, will lead them to spring
waters of Life. And God will wipe every last tear from their eyes."*
Revelation 7:17 MESSAGE

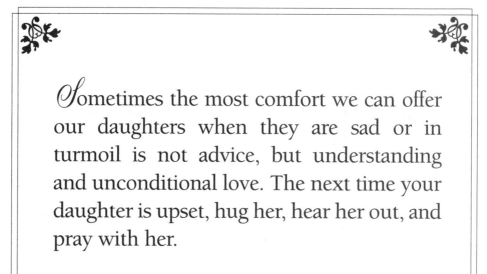

Sometimes the most comfort we can offer our daughters when they are sad or in turmoil is not advice, but understanding and unconditional love. The next time your daughter is upset, hug her, hear her out, and pray with her.

*G*od does not comfort us to make us
comfortable, but to make us comforters.

J. H. JOWLETT

*"Praise be to the God...who comforts us in all our troubles,
so that we can comfort those in any trouble with the comfort
we ourselves have received from God."*
2 Corinthians 1:3,4 NIV

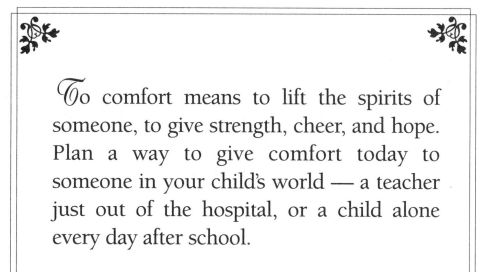

To comfort means to lift the spirits of someone, to give strength, cheer, and hope. Plan a way to give comfort today to someone in your child's world — a teacher just out of the hospital, or a child alone every day after school.

*O*ne of the biggest challenges for parents
is to help our junior high and high school
students develop critical thinking skills and
keep an open dialogue with them about
the issues and situations they face.

WENDY FLINT

*"The wisdom that comes from heaven is first of all pure; then peace-loving,
considerate, submissive, full of mercy and good fruit, impartial and sincere."*
James 3:17 NIV

When your children make statements and act contrary to the values they have been taught:

- Reason with them instead of overreacting.
- Help them think it through by asking questions.
- Encourage them to talk to God about it.

Remember, if we do all their thinking and are so strict they can't grow, we may drive them away from our home and from God.

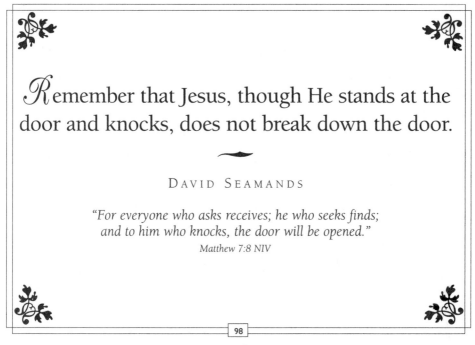

*R*emember that Jesus, though He stands at the door and knocks, does not break down the door.

DAVID SEAMANDS

"For everyone who asks receives; he who seeks finds;
and to him who knocks, the door will be opened."
Matthew 7:8 NIV

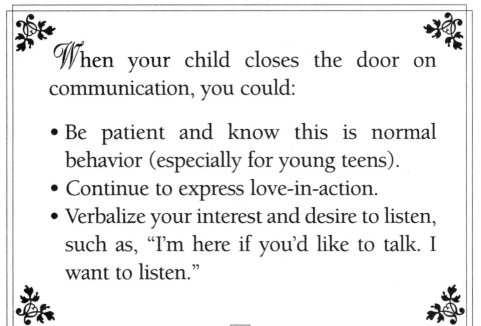

*W*hen your child closes the door on communication, you could:

- Be patient and know this is normal behavior (especially for young teens).
- Continue to express love-in-action.
- Verbalize your interest and desire to listen, such as, "I'm here if you'd like to talk. I want to listen."

Just as love to God begins with listening
to His Word, so the beginning of love for
the brethren is learning to listen to them.
It is God's love for us that He not only gives
us His Word but also lends us His ear.

DIETRICH BONHOEFFER

"Lord, I lift my hands to heaven and implore your help. Oh, listen to my cry."
Psalm 28:2

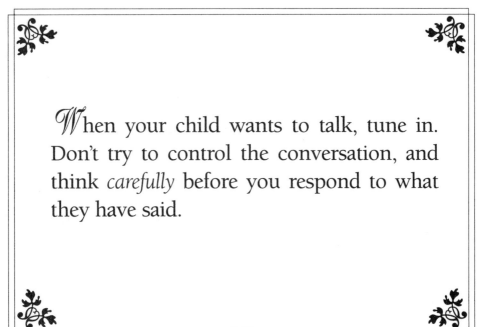

*W*hen your child wants to talk, tune in. Don't try to control the conversation, and think *carefully* before you respond to what they have said.

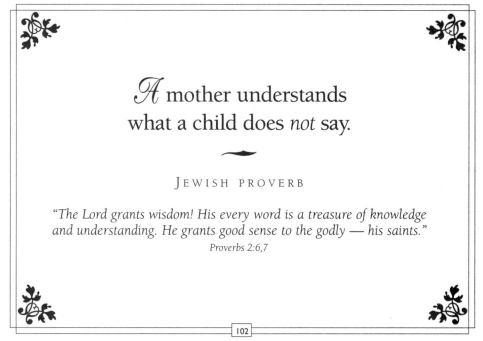

A mother understands
what a child does *not* say.

JEWISH PROVERB

*"The Lord grants wisdom! His every word is a treasure of knowledge
and understanding. He grants good sense to the godly — his saints."*
Proverbs 2:6,7

*W*hat is your child trying to say today in actions, attitudes, and expressions that they cannot say in words? Be sensitive to these nonverbal means of expression and pray for an understanding heart.

If Jesus Christ faced you squarely
with the question, "What do you want?"
what would you ask Him to do for you?
Then think of your children. What would
you want Jesus to do for each of them?
What request should you make for them?

JEAN FLEMING

"This is the confidence which we have before Him, that,
if we ask anything according to His will, He hears us.
And if we know that He hears us in whatever we ask, we know
that we have the requests which we have asked from Him."
1 John 5:14,15 NASB

During your quiet time, make prayers of those verses that converge with your children's needs and your hopes for them. For example:

- 1 Chronicles 29:19 (paraphrased) "Give my son a good heart toward You, God, so that he will want to obey You in the smallest detail."

- Proverbs 2:20 (paraphrased) "Lord, protect my daughter from friends that would lead her in the wrong direction; give her the right friends who would encourage her to excel and follow You."

We need to teach our kids
to dream with their eyes open.

CHERI FULLER

"A wise man thinks ahead."
Proverbs 13:16

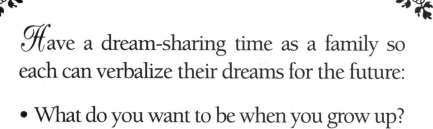

*H*ave a dream-sharing time as a family so each can verbalize their dreams for the future:

- What do you want to be when you grow up?
- What do you want out of life — travel, adventure, a big family?
- What can you see yourself doing in ten or twenty years?

Over a period of years, with Mother's constant encouragement, both Curtis and I started believing that we really could do anything we chose to do...that we were going to be extremely good and highly successful at whatever we attempted. Even today I can clearly hear her voice in the back of my head saying, "Bennie, you can do it. Don't you stop believing that for one second," "You weren't born to be a failure, Bennie," or one of her favorites: "You just ask the Lord, and He'll help you."

BEN CARSON, M.D.

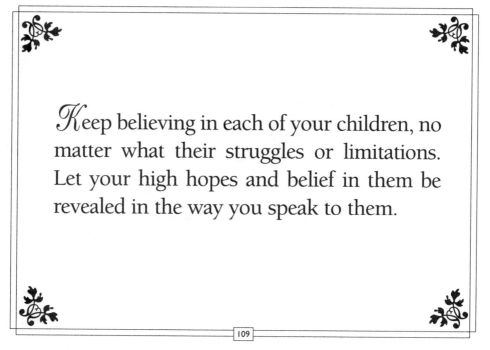

Keep believing in each of your children, no matter what their struggles or limitations. Let your high hopes and belief in them be revealed in the way you speak to them.

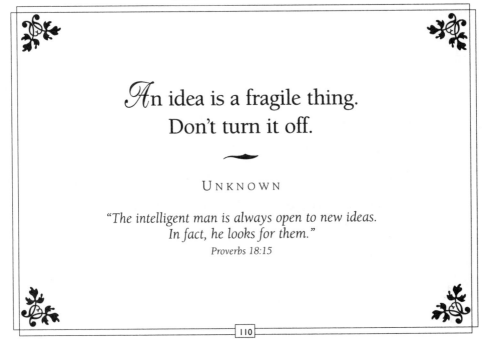

*A*n idea is a fragile thing.
Don't turn it off.

UNKNOWN

*"The intelligent man is always open to new ideas.
In fact, he looks for them."*
Proverbs 18:15

If your child has a "bright idea" this week, think about how you can turn it *on* instead of turning it off. If there is no time to work on it today, have them write it on an index card and tack it on the bulletin board under "Things to Do." You could also brainstorm about the materials they would need to carry out their idea and take them to the library to get more information.

𝒫lay is often talked about as if it were a relief from serious learning. But for children, play is serious learning. Play is really the work of childhood.

MR. (FRED) ROGERS

"Even a child is known by his actions, by whether his conduct is pure and right."
Proverbs 20:11 NIV

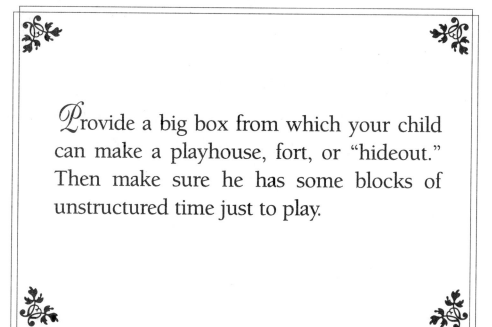

𝒫rovide a big box from which your child can make a playhouse, fort, or "hideout." Then make sure he has some blocks of unstructured time just to play.

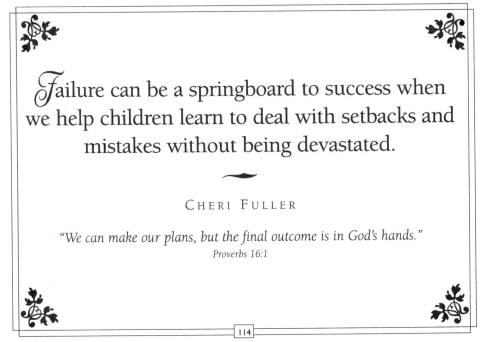

$\mathcal{F}$ailure can be a springboard to success when we help children learn to deal with setbacks and mistakes without being devastated.

CHERI FULLER

"We can make our plans, but the final outcome is in God's hands."
Proverbs 16:1

When an experiment or project doesn't work, say, "It's okay, because scientists fail their way to success. Take Jonas Salk, who failed countless times before finding the polio vaccine, or Thomas Edison, who failed hundreds of times before he invented the light bulb." Whether it's a failing test grade after studying hard or not making the soccer team, assure your child that they are a loved, worthwhile member of the family, that you are proud of their efforts. Finally, help them ask, "What can I learn from this?" and go on.

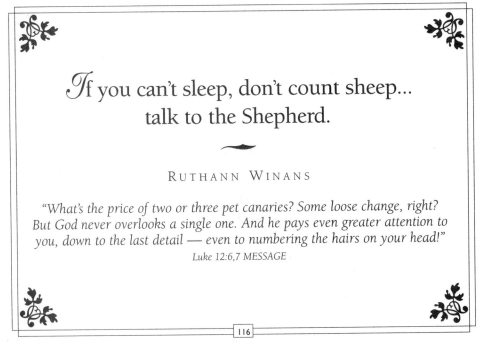

If you can't sleep, don't count sheep...
talk to the Shepherd.

RUTHANN WINANS

"What's the price of two or three pet canaries? Some loose change, right?
But God never overlooks a single one. And he pays even greater attention to
you, down to the last detail — even to numbering the hairs on your head!"
Luke 12:6,7 MESSAGE

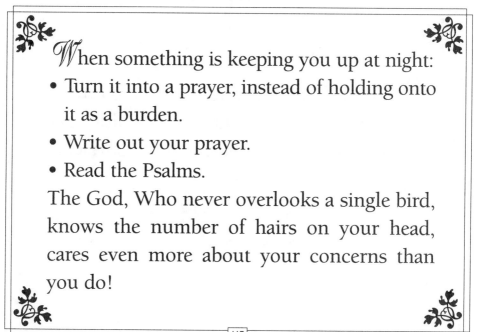

When something is keeping you up at night:

- Turn it into a prayer, instead of holding onto it as a burden.
- Write out your prayer.
- Read the Psalms.

The God, Who never overlooks a single bird, knows the number of hairs on your head, cares even more about your concerns than you do!

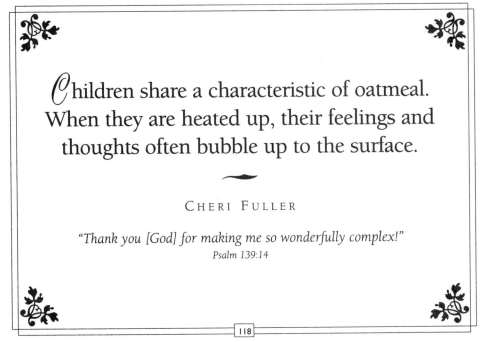

*C*hildren share a characteristic of oatmeal. When they are heated up, their feelings and thoughts often bubble up to the surface.

CHERI FULLER

"Thank you [God] for making me so wonderfully complex!"
Psalm 139:14

$\mathcal{G}$et your child heated up on a regular basis by engaging him physically: Throw the football or baseball, play ping pong, or take a brisk walk — great stimulators to communication!

Take a moment to listen today
to what your children are trying to say.
Listen today, whatever you do
and they will come back to listen to you.

UNKNOWN

*"Wisdom and good judgment live together, for wisdom knows
where to discover knowledge and understanding."*
Proverbs 8:12

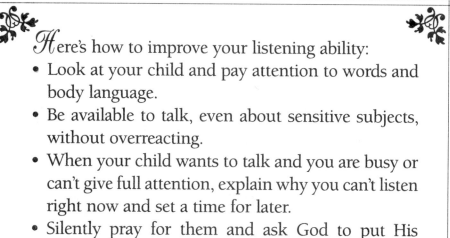

*H*ere's how to improve your listening ability:

- Look at your child and pay attention to words and body language.
- Be available to talk, even about sensitive subjects, without overreacting.
- When your child wants to talk and you are busy or can't give full attention, explain why you can't listen right now and set a time for later.
- Silently pray for them and ask God to put His thoughts in your mind and show you how to respond to what they say.

One way to cultivate a taste for Christian music in your children is through sharing a testimony song. This is a song that expresses your love for God and describes your walk with the Lord.... It lets someone else understand why you love Jesus. Every Christian should have a testimony song.

AL MENCONI

"Let everything you do reflect your love of the truth and the fact that you are in dead earnest about it."

Titus 2:7

$\mathscr{A}$sk your child for five minutes of their time. Show them a song that means a lot to you and have them read the lyrics while you play the song. Then ask them to play a song that has meaning to them.

Motherhood 101

As our children grow and we gradually lose direct control — as their wings get stronger and they begin to fly out of the nest for short flights and then to college and beyond, our prayers are the wind beneath their wings.

CHERI FULLER

"Know the God of your father, and serve Him with a whole heart and a willing mind; for the Lord searches all hearts, and understands every intent of the thoughts."
1 Chronicles 28:9 NASB

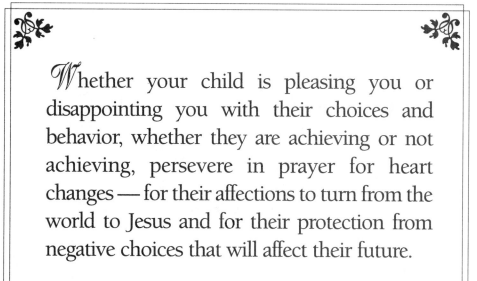

Whether your child is pleasing you or disappointing you with their choices and behavior, whether they are achieving or not achieving, persevere in prayer for heart changes — for their affections to turn from the world to Jesus and for their protection from negative choices that will affect their future.

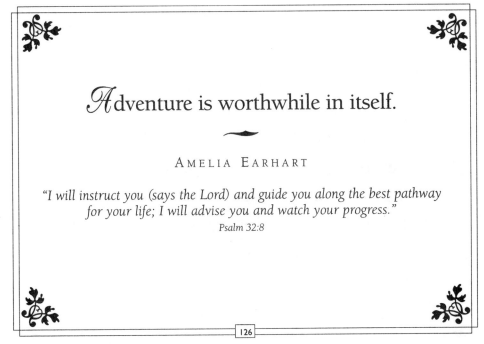

Adventure is worthwhile in itself.

AMELIA EARHART

"I will instruct you (says the Lord) and guide you along the best pathway for your life; I will advise you and watch your progress."

Psalm 32:8

*T*alk with your children about an adventure they've always wanted to have: climbing a mountain, an overnight hike, or whatever their definition of "adventure" is. Help them visualize their adventure. Encourage them to read about it, save toward it, and look forward to pursuing that adventure.

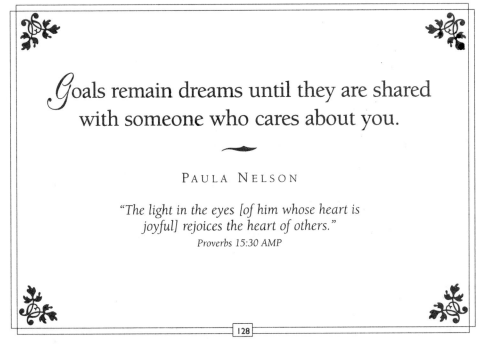

*G*oals remain dreams until they are shared
with someone who cares about you.

PAULA NELSON

*"The light in the eyes [of him whose heart is
joyful] rejoices the heart of others."*
Proverbs 15:30 AMP

$\mathscr{T}$alk with your child about the future. What are their hopes and dreams? How can you help them set, plan and work toward goals (such as taking courses at school and getting experience in the community) that will lead them where they want to go. Sharing goals and hearing encouragement from others not only brings accountability into the equation, it brings dreams to *life*.

*S*he always leaned to watch for us,
Anxious if we were late,
In the winter by the window,
In the summer by the gate.

MARGARET WIDDEMER

*"Yes, Lord, let your constant love surround us,
for our hopes are in you alone."*
Psalm 33:22

*C*hildren need us at the most unpredictable and often inconvenient times — sometimes right after school, or at midnight after a date. *Purpose* to be there — available, listening, and caring. This is when they open up and talk about their thoughts, feelings, hurts, and dreams. These are "prime times" in communication for parents. Don't miss them!

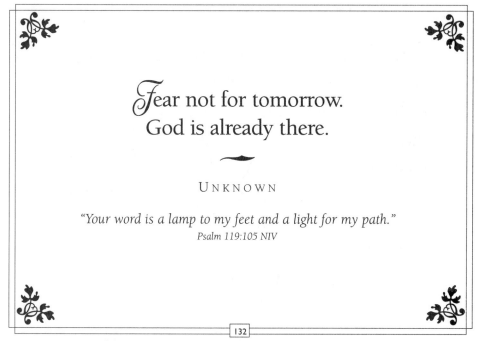

Fear not for tomorrow.
God is already there.

UNKNOWN

"Your word is a lamp to my feet and a light for my path."
Psalm 119:105 NIV

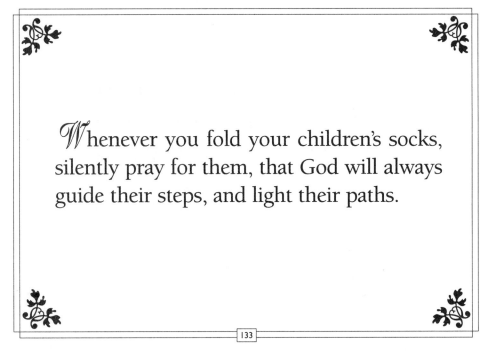

*W*henever you fold your children's socks, silently pray for them, that God will always guide their steps, and light their paths.

Tie the child to you, and the child
will either run away or turn into a stone.
Give the child wings, and the child will
use them to fly back to you.

ANGELA BARRON MCBRIDE

*"Young man, it's wonderful to be young! Enjoy every minute of it!
Do all you want to; take in everything, but realize that you must
account to God for everything you do."*
Ecclesiastes 11:9

    *L*et your older children know that you are preparing them for when they will be on their own. Teach them how to manage money by helping them open a checking account. Let them learn to deal with their own responsibilities and mistakes by not rushing down to the high school with the research paper or lunch money they forgot.

Children's lives are our garden. They will remain a garden, as distinct from a wilderness, only if someone cultivates them. But they bear witness to God's glory in the very fact that they need this cultivation, this "weeding and pruning;" for like a garden, they teem with life. And, like a garden, they will surpass our expectations for them if they are enabled to do so.

MARTI GARLETT

"The old life is a grass life, its beauty is short-lived as wildflowers;
Grass dries up, flowers droop, God's Word goes on and on forever."
1 Peter 1:23,24 MESSAGE

*O*ne of the best ways to cultivate the garden of your child's life is to recognize learning differences and patterns, and teach in ways that help concepts "click." If reading the chapter assigned doesn't work, tape-record it, so they can listen to it and follow along. If they don't memorize the multiplication tables as fast as the other kids, let them practice them orally while bouncing the basketball.

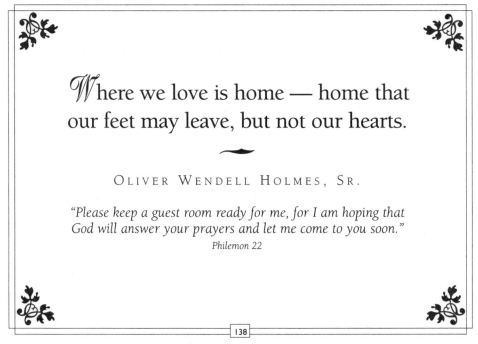

Where we love is home — home that our feet may leave, but not our hearts.

OLIVER WENDELL HOLMES, SR.

"Please keep a guest room ready for me, for I am hoping that God will answer your prayers and let me come to you soon."
Philemon 22

About the time you get through your sadness over their departure, your college student comes back! The first summer after college can be a little rocky. Here's how to smooth it out:

- Talk together and set up some guidelines on important daily issues (laundry, hours, etc.).
- Try to meet occasionally for a meal and togetherness.
- Be patient when you see changes in your child you didn't "order." Accept and love them.
- Be spontaneous and make some memories; the summer will fly!

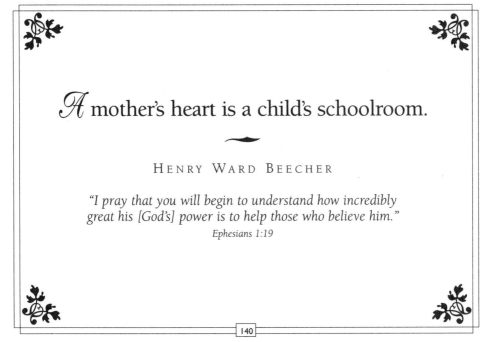

A mother's heart is a child's schoolroom.

HENRY WARD BEECHER

"I pray that you will begin to understand how incredibly great his [God's] power is to help those who believe him."
Ephesians 1:19

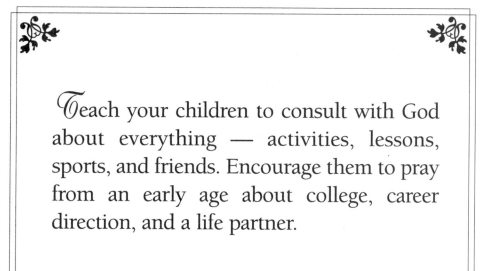

Teach your children to consult with God about everything — activities, lessons, sports, and friends. Encourage them to pray from an early age about college, career direction, and a life partner.

*T*oo many people put off something that brings them joy just because they didn't have it on their schedule, didn't know it was coming, or are too rigid to depart from the routine.

ERMA BOMBECK

"Do not withhold good from those who deserve it, when it is in your power to act."
Proverbs 3:27 NIV

*W*hen your child or teen says, "Let's go to the mall!" or "Let's stay home, pop some popcorn, and watch an old movie together," or "Let's play cards or a board game," or "Let's go the lake and rollerblade!" *seize the moment* (especially if you have rollerblades) and enjoy the time together. Instead of giving excuses, do it now!

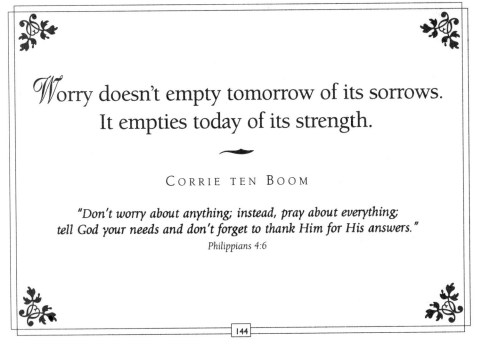

Worry doesn't empty tomorrow of its sorrows.
It empties today of its strength.

CORRIE TEN BOOM

*"Don't worry about anything; instead, pray about everything;
tell God your needs and don't forget to thank Him for His answers."*
Philippians 4:6

*E*mpty out any worries you have today concerning finances, health, children, or anything else. In your mind's eye, think of pouring them all out, as from a pitcher, right at the feet of Jesus. Now let your pitcher refill with His peace and love.

When teenagers are pulling away and pushing the limits, often the parent pulls away or distances herself. But it is important for parents not to pull away or sever the relationship! Adolescents are not ready for complete emotional or financial independence.

ADELE FABER

"How happy I am to find some of your children here, and to see that they are living as they should, following the Truth, obeying God's command."
2 John 4

*P*icture your parent-teen relationship like two people at the end of a rope, each tugging. If you keep tugging and they do, you get closer to the middle. If you let go of the rope, they fall down and are headed for trouble. Worse, the teen ends up feeling, "My parents don't care about me." Keep holding *your* end of the rope!

*W*ords have the power to boost or deflate a child's self-worth, to hurt or inspire him, to cheer or to discourage him. Choose your words wisely!

CHERI FULLER

"Death and life are in the power of the tongue."
Proverbs 18:21 NASB

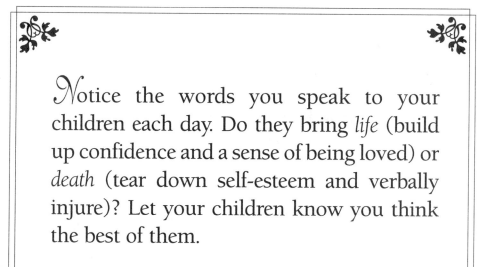

Notice the words you speak to your children each day. Do they bring *life* (build up confidence and a sense of being loved) or *death* (tear down self-esteem and verbally injure)? Let your children know you think the best of them.

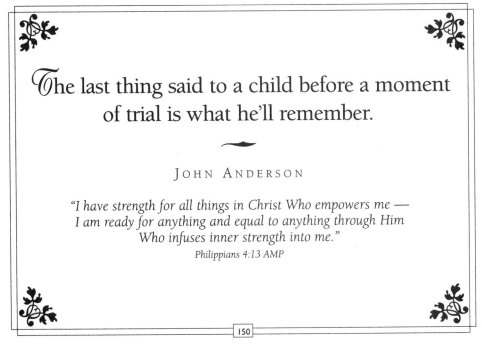

The last thing said to a child before a moment of trial is what he'll remember.

JOHN ANDERSON

"I have strength for all things in Christ Who empowers me —
I am ready for anything and equal to anything through Him
Who infuses inner strength into me."
Philippians 4:13 AMP

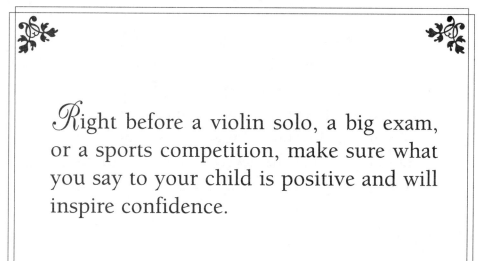

$\mathscr{R}$ight before a violin solo, a big exam, or a sports competition, make sure what you say to your child is positive and will inspire confidence.

I did not have my mother long, but she cast over me an influence which lasted all my life.... If it had not been for her appreciation and her faith in me at a critical time in my experience, I should never likely have become an inventor. I was always a careless boy.... But her firmness, her sweetness, her goodness, were potent powers to keep me in the right path.

THOMAS A. EDISON

"I will try to walk a blameless path, but how I need your help, especially in my own home, where I long to act as I should."
Psalm 101:2

Some of a child's most challenging experiences can bring out their greatest strengths as an adult. Show faith in your child and in their gifts — determination, curiosity, logic, resourcefulness, and creativity. Keep believing in them even if no one else does. You never know, you may have another "Edison" in your home when they grow into their gifts!

In search of my mother's garden,
I found my own.

ALICE WALKER

*"He's using you, fitting you in brick by brick, stone by stone,
with Christ Jesus as the cornerstone that holds all the parts together.
We see it taking shape day after day — a holy temple built by God,
all of us built into it, a temple in which God is quite at home."*
Ephesians 2:21,22 MESSAGE

Take a look at your calendar. Is there any empty space? Is there any blank space for just being together, stopping to smell the flowers in your garden, enjoying something about which you are passionate, or just sitting by the fire to read or talk? Share that time and your love with someone precious to you.

When our youngest son went off to college...we were unprepared for the ache of parting. When we parents say, "Someday you'll grow up," we mean a day in the far-distant future. Not today! The bittersweet truth is: That day comes much too soon.

MARY JANE CHAMBERS

"Little children, let us stop just <u>saying</u> we love people, let us <u>really</u> love them, and <u>show it</u> by our actions."
1 John 3:18

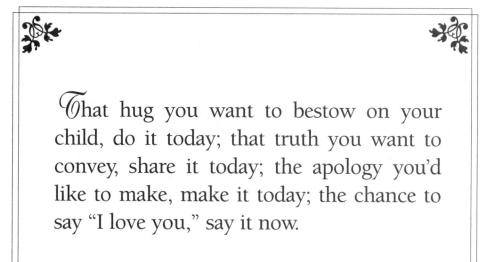

That hug you want to bestow on your child, do it today; that truth you want to convey, share it today; the apology you'd like to make, make it today; the chance to say "I love you," say it now.

References

About the Author

Cheri Fuller is a wife, a mother of three grown children, a dynamic speaker, and author of fourteen books. She holds a B. A. in English and History and a Master's Degree in English Literature. She is a contributing editor for *Today's Christian Woman* magazine. Besides being interviewed by hundreds of radio stations in the U.S. and writing articles for numerous national magazines, Cheri has served as a consultant and national spokesperson for MCI. She and her family live in Oklahoma City, Oklahoma.

Additional Honor Book titles by Cheri Fuller include:

Motivating Your Kids From Crayons to Career
Home Life: The Key to Your Child's Success at School
Christmas Treasures of the Heart

Other books by Cheri Fuller:

Trading Your Worry for Wonder
Unlocking Your Child's Learning Potential
Home Business Happiness
365 Ways to Build Your Child's Self-Esteem

To contact her, write:
Cheri Fuller
P.O. Box 770493
Oklahoma City, Oklahoma 73177